Rescued Images

Memories of a Childhood in Hiding

Editors: Stuart Waldman and Elizabeth Mann
Design: Lesley Ehlers Design

Prints of collages by Ralph Salamone at Chelsea Crossings
Sag Harbor, New York

Library of Congress Cataloging-in-Publication Data

Jacobsen, Ruth, 1932-
    Rescued images : memories of a childhood in hiding / Ruth Jacobsen
        p. cm
    ISBN 1-931414-00-9
    1. Jacobsen, Ruth, 1932—Juvenile literature. 2. Jewish children in the
Holocaust—Netherlands—Biography—Juvenile literature. 3. Holocaust, Jewish
(1939-1945)—Netherlands—Personal narratives—Juvenile literature. 4. Jews,
German—Netherlands—Biography—Juvenile literature. 5.
Netherlands—Biography—Juvenile literature. [1. Jacobsen, Ruth, 1932—Childhood and
youth. 2. Jews—Netherlands. 3. Holocaust survivors.] 1. Title.

DS135.N6J33 2001
940.53'18'092—dc21

                                                    2001030298

Printed in China

der elegante mit gräflicher Krone versehene Pack- u. Livagen. Ein
livrierter Chauffeur führ uns in ein romantisch schönes Schloss. Dieser massive Steinbau ist ringsum von Wasser umgeben, worin seinerzeit die herrlichsten Seerosen blühten. Alle Einzelheiten zu beschreiben würde zu weitführen und will ich mich auf ein Minimum beschränken, damit Ihr Euch ein annäherndes Bild machen könnt. In diesem Schloss wohnten wir die ersten zehn Tage. Wir saßen auch schon direkt zum Dinner im großen Speisesaal, dessen Wände ringsum mit lebensgrossen Ahnenbilder geschmückt sind, an einer Tafel von zu Personen, die sich natürlich nur aus Baronen und Grafen zusammensetzte, die teilweise zu Gast dort waren. Am Tisch wurde holl., engl., franz., dänisch und deutsch gesprochen, doch herrschte ein vollkommen zwangloser Ton. Wir kamen uns vor wie in einem Traum und ich musste michals- mal in den Arm kneifen, ob ich das wirklich wäre, die als Gast- dame zur Rechten des Herrn Baron, als Erste von dem weissbe- handschuhten Diener die auserlesensten Speisen, dessen Folge nicht enden wollte, vorgelegt bekam. Es war eine Freude zu sehen, wie Ruth mit einer Selbstverständlichkeit, also ganz Dame, an der Tafel sass, als hätte sie ihr Lebtag noch nichts anderes vor sich gese- hen. Wir konnten stolz darauf sein. Nun erst einmal zu den Leuten selbst. Der Herr Baron zählt zu den fünf grössten Per

Rescued Images

Memories of a Childhood in Hiding

Ruth Jacobsen

MIKAYA PRESS

NEW YORK

Dedicated to my mother and
father. They survived the war but
could not speak about it.
I found my voice and have tried to
speak for them as well as myself.

Amsterdam

Oud Zuylen
Utrecht

Holland

Rotterdam

Germany

Roermond

Düsseldorf

Belgium

Frankenberg

Brunssum

Heerlen

My mother told me this. When I was four years old, I was standing at the top of the steps of our house in Frankenberg, Germany. A bunch of young children were yelling at me: "Juden Stinker, Juden Stinker." My mother ran outside when she heard them. She saw me standing there, facing them and yelling back "Juden Stinker," having no idea what it meant.

When I was ten, I became a "hidden child." For two and a half years, I was hidden from the Nazis in the homes of strangers who had the courage to take me in. After the war, when I heard of the horrors people experienced in concentration camps, I felt that in comparison I had it easy. It took me many years to realize that my own life had been shattered.

Even after I emigrated to the United States I did not talk with my relatives there about the war years, and they never asked.

When my family fled Germany in 1939 we had to leave everything behind. Our landlady in Düsseldorf sent our trunks to us in Holland. We only received one of them, but in it were, among other things, our family photo albums.

In 1942, when we were forced into hiding, we again had to leave everything behind. Cees van Bart, a Dutch neighbor, entered our house after the Germans had sealed it off to rescue things that were of value to us. He took his life in his hands. If he had been caught, he and his family could have been shot or sent to a concentration camp. He found the photo albums and hid them in his house. When the war ended he presented them to us.

When I emigrated to America I took the albums with me. They remained packed in a box for about forty years. I knew they were there, but could not look at them.

For years, as an artist, I created books of collages, mixing photographs and paint. Many of the images I used in my first books were of people in war and turmoil. Their agony moved me.

One day I found the courage to pick up the albums. My fear had always been that I would break down or become hysterical at seeing my parents' images again. Finally I was able to put aside the fears I had felt for so many years and look at them.

The photographs evoked feelings I could only express in collage form. I needed to move the photographs out of the albums and into my life. I used the original photographs, as well as letters, other images, and acrylic paints to create collages. In the process of working with them, more and more of the past came back. I began to remember . . .

Flight

My mother was born in the village of Frankenberg, Germany, and so was I. Her parents owned a shoe store, which she inherited after their death. In 1937, when Jews were no longer allowed to own anything, my mother was forced to sell the store to the German government for a ridiculously low price. We moved to Düsseldorf.

Instead of a house in a small, familiar village, we now lived in an apartment in a big city. I had to memorize the address, and I remember it still: *Grafenberger Allee 101.*

It was in Düsseldorf that I met my first toad. I was about six years old. Our landlady kept a toad in an aquarium. I loved to watch him. He sat motionless while we stared at each other. Then suddenly I would see him land at the far end of his aquarium. I could never catch that split second when he started to jump, only his landing on the other side. I was convinced he knew when I was going to blink my eyes and he jumped at that very moment.

The toad liked live insects, so my father taught me how to catch flies. The fly had to be on a flat surface. With my hand half closed, I would swiftly swipe from the back to the front, while closing my hand into a tight fist. The fly would buzz, tickling the inside of my hand. Then I would lift the top of the aquarium a crack and release it inside. The toad would catch it in flight by quickly rolling out his sticky tongue. He would curl his tongue back into his mouth and gulp down the whole fly. I became so good at catching flies that the landlady requested my services. I caught all available flies and kept them in a jar.

My father's parents lived near Düsseldorf and we visited them frequently. They had

been friends with a Dutch baron and his wife since the 1920s. When the Nazi persecution of the Jews became worse, the baron and his wife promised my grandparents and their family a safe haven with them in Holland.

On November 9, 1938, our landlady, a Christian, told us that the Nazis were going to raid all Jewish homes that night and round up men, women, and children. My parents and I walked all night, afraid to go home. As we walked we saw glass, furniture, and even people being thrown out of windows. I remember the sound of crashing objects and a thick blanket of fear surrounding us. It was called *Kristallnacht:* The Night of Broken Glass.

In 1939, my parents and I fled from Germany to Holland by train. My grandfather was too ill to travel and my grandmother remained behind with him in Düsseldorf. We didn't carry suitcases—that could have aroused suspicions. Instead, my parents, my doll, Ellen, and I all wore two layers of clothing. I could feel my parents' anxiety during the train ride. If the Germans had demanded our identity papers, they would have discovered that we were Jewish and we would have been sent back to Germany.

While we were on the train, my mother told me that I was going to meet a baron, a baroness, and their two teenage daughters. To show my respect, I had to learn how to curtsy when meeting them. I had to practice. With thumbs and forefingers I held my dress by the hem, extending it out to the sides as far as it would go. Then with my right foot forward, in a quick motion I slightly bent both knees. It felt demeaning to me, but fortunately I only had to do it once.

When we arrived in the city of Utrecht in Holland, a limousine was waiting for us. On the door was painted the family crest, and inside were the baroness, one daughter, and a chauffeur in a uniform. We were driven to a fourteenth-century castle surrounded by a moat. There we were the guests of Baron and Baroness van Tuyll van Serooskerken.

The castle was located in Oud Zuylen, a village a few miles north of Utrecht. Since the whole village belonged to the baron's family, every house had shutters bearing their family crest.

The river Vecht wound its way through the village. Barges and houseboats passed under a small drawbridge. At the sound of horns from approaching boats the operator would open the bridge and lower a long pole with an open canvas pouch on the end. The owner of the boat would drop his fee for crossing under the bridge into the pouch.

I loved to sit at the river's edge watching the houseboats. I could see moments in the life of a family sliding by. Children and dogs were playing on deck. A woman was hanging the laundry on a line. I wondered what the inside looked like.

The grounds around the castle were beautiful. Every evening after dinner my

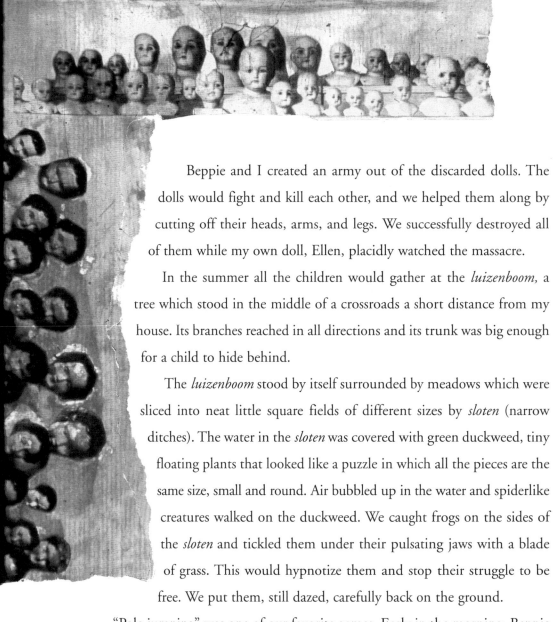

Beppie and I created an army out of the discarded dolls. The dolls would fight and kill each other, and we helped them along by cutting off their heads, arms, and legs. We successfully destroyed all of them while my own doll, Ellen, placidly watched the massacre.

In the summer all the children would gather at the *luizenboom,* a tree which stood in the middle of a crossroads a short distance from my house. Its branches reached in all directions and its trunk was big enough for a child to hide behind.

The *luizenboom* stood by itself surrounded by meadows which were sliced into neat little square fields of different sizes by *sloten* (narrow ditches). The water in the *sloten* was covered with green duckweed, tiny floating plants that looked like a puzzle in which all the pieces are the same size, small and round. Air bubbled up in the water and spiderlike creatures walked on the duckweed. We caught frogs on the sides of the *sloten* and tickled them under their pulsating jaws with a blade of grass. This would hypnotize them and stop their struggle to be free. We put them, still dazed, carefully back on the ground.

"Pole jumping" was one of our favorite games. Early in the morning, Beppie would be outside my house calling, "Ha Rrrrrroeti," rolling his Rs with such full and long trills that even my mother started calling me that way. (Roeti in Dutch sounds like Ruty).

Beppie brought poles, about five feet long, for each of us. Taking a pole and holding it straight out in front with both hands, we ran as fast as we could and thrust it as far out into the water as we could reach. Like pole vaulters, we flung ourselves to the other side. When we pulled the pole out, duckweed clung to it, magically glistening in the sun. The gap in the duckweed would close again. This is how we traveled from *sloot* to *sloot*. It was not easy to reach the other side without losing a wooden shoe and sinking in the mud. Sometimes we landed in our socks in the mud on the banks of the ditches. Beppie's mother had warned him not to come home in wet and muddy socks, but it happened so regularly that he had to develop a system. We took off our socks, washed them, wrung them out, and then slapped them on a flat rock until they were almost dry. By the time we got home the socks were clean and just a little damp.

For the first couple of months that we were in Holland the one sentence I knew was *kan niet verstaan* (I cannot understand). When I started to go to school my feeling of surprise at hearing people speak in that strange guttural language disappeared.

I learned Dutch very quickly. I spoke with barely an accent and I even performed in school plays. I also looked Dutch, with my round red cheeks and blue eyes. I was comfortable walking and even dancing in wooden shoes. They were wonderful to wear in the winter. Besides being warm, when the snow had the right consistency, it would pack under each wooden sole, making you taller and taller until you fell down and had to scrape off the snow.

The house we lived in was right next to the elementary school. A fancy wrought iron fence separated our backyard from the school's playground. Someone had bent two of the rods slightly apart so a child could just wriggle through. Every day I would wait at home until the school bell rang, then run outside, slip through the bars, and still be in time for the lineup in the schoolyard.

My father had a swing, bars, and rings installed for me in our backyard. Sand was dumped in front of it. After school and at lunchtime children came to our yard and we competed in doing tricks on the bars and rings.

I liked the swing the best. We would swing as high as we dared, then jump off and mark the place in the sand where we landed. The next person would try to go even higher and jump further. The exhilaration of jumping off a moving swing into the air . . . just letting go . . . is still with me. This whole time felt free and full of excitement.

War

May 10, 1940. I was eight when the German troops marched through Oud Zuylen. They had defeated the Dutch army and bombed Rotterdam, one of the largest ports in Europe. My parents had intended to leave Holland for America, but now that the port was destroyed, we could not go.

The day was full of bright sunshine, but the shutters of the houses and the shops were closed as if it were nighttime. Everyone stayed indoors. The streets were empty.

The house was dark in the middle of the day. As I looked through a crack in the shutters, I saw the Dutch soldiers who had been taken prisoner, looking bedraggled and defeated as they trailed behind their crisp, goose-stepping captors.

As they passed our house the Germans were singing the songs I knew well. They were the same songs my mother had taught me in Germany. She loved to sing, especially while cleaning the house. I carried a small basket and trailed behind her, imitating her cleaning as well as her singing. That day the songs sounded dark and frightening.

Looking at photographs from that time, I see a round-faced, sturdy little girl with an open look in her eyes. On my coat is pinned the letter R. At that time, stores sold alphabet pins made of phosphorescent material that glowed in the dark. Children bought the first letter of their names.

We were living under "blackout" rules. Every night streetlights were turned off and curtains were drawn. The darkness made it impossible for the British air force to find and bomb German military installations. When we played outside in the pitch darkness, we saw only the glowing letters dancing, disconnected from our bodies.

The German soldiers established their headquarters in our small village. I started to hang around their quarters to hear them sing the familiar folk songs. The soldiers were young and friendly. After a while they invited me inside. I spoke German and had no inhibitions. I sang the songs my mother had taught me, everything from sentimental love songs to World War I battle songs. They were delighted and invited me to sit on their knees, encouraging me to sing more. I loved their applause. I didn't connect the goose-stepping, hard-faced invaders with these easygoing young soldiers. I didn't even think it particularly strange to have soldiers stationed in Oud Zuylen. I just liked singing in German.

My life was uninterrupted. I went to school next door, and played outside during the summer.

Across the street from our house lay a small wooded area and beyond that flowed the river Vecht where a houseboat was moored. I was fascinated by it. The outside was freshly painted in bright colors and the windows had neat shutters that were closed at night. The boat was so small and low it seemed to me that only little people could live there, but I saw a very tall man enter it regularly. He had to duck his head in order to go through the door. A woman lived there as well, though she had no trouble getting in. As I watched them, I tried to imagine what the inside of their boat looked like.

They must have noticed me, because one day they invited me to come in. I was very excited. The inside was very long. The kitchen came first, then the living room and bedroom, all in a row. Through the windows, I saw water on three sides. As I walked through the rooms, I felt the water moving underneath and the whole boat slightly rocking from side to side. I heard the water softly lapping.

Sometimes the couple would go on vacation in their houseboat, leaving its usual space empty. Eagerly I would wait for their return. In the winter, when the water was frozen over, the houseboat could not move. Then when I visited, it felt as steady as my own home. You could step outside right onto the ice or climb out a window and walk around the whole boat.

Every time I visited I was given a large bowl of oatmeal cooked in buttermilk, a typical Dutch dish. In the winter it was served hot and in the summer cold. A jar of *stroop,* a sweet syrup that tasted like molasses, sat on the table. They let me spoon out the *stroop* myself. Very slowly I let it dribble from the spoon onto the oatmeal, writing my name with it and making lots of swirls. I loved it.

One day when I arrived the woman was crying. She told me she was leaving in the houseboat for good. I was very upset and asked my parents why she had to leave. They told me her husband had been killed in the war.

How could such a strong, tall man die? The word "war," so often mentioned by my parents, now had a meaning, and it frightened me.

~~~~~~~~

My grandfather had died of another stroke and my grandmother came to live with us in Holland. Though I remember my grandfather clearly and fondly, I was not close to my grandmother. I remember very little about her stay, just her shrill voice and everyone quarreling with each other constantly. One day, about a year after she arrived, my grandmother received a letter from the Germans telling her to come to their offices to register. It was signed by both a German and someone with an obviously Jewish name. The Jewish name made us think it was safe for her to go. My grandmother never came back.

Jews who co-signed such letters were led to believe they would be saved from persecution in exchange for the Jews they trapped in this way. Of course when their usefulness ended, the Germans exterminated them.

After the war we found out that my grandmother and many other Jews had been packed into a train like cattle and sent to a concentration camp. Too old and weak to survive the terrible conditions on the train, she died en route.

As soon as my grandmother disappeared, my parents began planning for us to go into hiding.

The Yellow Star

I was nine when the yellow star changed my life. I recognized the work my mother put into making the stitches even and perfect as she sewed the stars on all our outer garments. The Germans gave precise instructions about exactly where to sew the star. It had to be visible to everyone at first glance.

When I wore the yellow star, I felt a mixture of pride and shame. My mother's sewing was perfect, yet I wanted to cover it up. Even strangers immediately could see that I was Jewish. Sometimes I saw pity or hatred on their faces.

Everything changed quickly. The Nazis created schools for Jewish children only. All Jewish children were pulled out of their local schools and ordered to go to a central location.

Now, instead of slipping through the fence, I was forced to travel by bus to a school in Utrecht. Every morning I waited for the bus with adults who were going to work. It was winter and we huddled under a flimsy shelter that never really protected us from the cold and rain.

One day a group of boys from the Dutch Hitler Youth got into the bus. When they saw my yellow star they demanded my seat even though the bus was half empty. Everybody looked uncomfortable but no one dared to interfere. The boys were rough and rowdy and felt their power. I remained seated, immobilized with fear, not comprehending the fury they directed at me.

One of the passengers motioned to me. I left my seat and went to her.

Without words she pointed to her lap where I was to sit for the rest of the trip. I sat as far forward as I could, holding on to my schoolbag, my feet not touching the floor. I was embarrassed to be sitting on a stranger's lap. The bus was quiet. No one challenged the boys or even looked at them.

I never told my parents.

~~~~~~~~

Fewer and fewer pupils came to class at the all-Jewish school. When I told my parents they became very upset. They made me promise to count the students every day. When only a certain number were left, I was to stay home. I was quite happy with that prospect and every day brought home the latest count. I didn't know then that each disappearance meant another family had been deported to a concentration camp.

The day finally came when I stayed at home. Instead of feeling happy that I did not have to go to school anymore, I was frightened. Something was wrong. Everyday routines were gone and nobody could relax.

In Hiding

One day, while playing outside, I was called into the house.

Three suitcases were packed. With my doll, Ellen, in my arms, I walked out of the house with my mother and father, never to return again. We walked across the street to another house, up the stairs, and into a room. I was told to stay behind the curtains so no one could see me. Through the smallest crack I looked down and saw the same friends I had been playing with minutes before continuing their game.

We took the yellow stars from our coats and burned them in an ashtray, watching their slow disintegration. We were in hiding.

No one was supposed to know we were there. When the owners of the house were not at home, we could not even flush the toilet. I was told only to whisper. My mother told me I even whispered when talking in my sleep.

Cees van Bart had found this hiding place for us. He and others who would move us again and again were part of the "Dutch Resistance" and spent the war secretly fighting the Nazis. Their anonymity had to be maintained. Except for Cees, I never knew their real names.

The Resistance decided it was too dangerous for us to stay in Oud Zuylen. Everybody knew us and just a glimpse would have given us, and the people who were hiding us, away. They also decided that it was safer to hide two people rather than three, so my family had to be split up. My parents could stay together, but they would never be able to go outside. With my blue eyes I didn't look "Jewish" by Hitler's definition and I spoke Dutch without an accent. I was allowed to go outside and even play with neighborhood children.

wwwwwww

Each time I was placed in a new home, I would have to learn all about the family's background so I could step into their life and assume my new identity. It was hard not to confuse the details of all the families.

My last name would change as I moved from family to family, but to make it a little easier for me I would be allowed to keep one first name. Ruth sounded too biblical and might have raised suspicions about my religion, so I had to choose a new first name. I chose Truusje, a good Dutch name. I became her and left Ruth in another life.

The Resistance taught me what I had to do to survive. I had to listen carefully to what they said. My life depended on it. If I didn't do exactly what they told me, I, as well as the family that was hiding me, would be picked up and sent to a concentration camp.

I learned that the questions I asked could not be answered. I did not ask questions anymore.

I learned to think before speaking. If I acted impulsively I might reveal that I really was Ruth.

I learned that, in any situation, most adults sided with their own children, even if they were wrong. I could not object.

I learned that when asked to do a chore, I could not object.

I learned I had to be well behaved at all times. The families that were hiding me had put themselves in great danger to protect me.

My knowledge of the war was simple:

S.S. officers were dangerous and ruthless.

The Allies were supposed to liberate us from the Germans.

The Dutch Resistance was helping us to survive.

If you were caught by the Germans or Dutch traitors you would be sent to a concentration camp to die.

My first year of hiding is a blur of feelings and incidents.

I found myself in a smoke-filled room with many young men and women. I was wearing a winter coat. A woman took my hand and we went up a long staircase to the attic. She told me I was in Amsterdam.

She took me to a bed and told me to go to sleep. The blackout was in effect, as it had been in Oud Zuylen, so I was not allowed to use any lights. I lay fully clothed on the bed afraid to move. There weren't any shadows or faint outlines of the attic room. I could only sense the rafters overhead and an enormous space surrounding me. I was in a large dark hole. I lay perfectly still and just waited.

The time passed and I heard the city waking up. Bicycles and cable cars clattered down below and people's voices drifted up in the early morning air. A gray light came through the windows. I was very cold, sick, and dazed. I could not believe that everything sounded so normal. People outside were talking as if nothing had happened.

<hr>

I stepped off a train with a woman who held my hand. We walked for a while and stopped in front of a house with a small gate. She told me to wait and continued to the front door. She talked to someone, came back, took my hand and told me the people had changed their minds about taking me. I didn't know why I was walking with this woman or why I had been rejected. I didn't want to stay with any of them.

At the next house, while I waited again outside, I looked through the window. Two girls were sitting by a Christmas tree opening their presents. A woman beckoned me to come to the door. She was willing to take me. Walking that small distance to the woman, I felt weary and lost. When I entered the house I was suddenly face to face with the girls I had watched from outside. I stood for a moment in the doorway of the warm room with my suitcase and my coat still on, watching them play with their new gifts. The mother interrupted them and introduced me. She told them I would be staying with them for a while. They looked up at me. She told them to share their presents with me. They looked at each other.

Was I to take off my coat, leave my suitcase, and join their intimate circle? I was not their friend—we didn't even know each other. What would I do with the gifts they might decide to give me? I just stood there.

Finally the mother took all of us upstairs to sleep. The bedroom was very dark. I was taken to a bed. Other people's lives surrounded me. I felt the clutter of their room and wondered how I was going to fit into it. I heard them sleep all night.

One of the girls was my age, the other a couple of years older. The older girl and her mother had terrible fights, yelling and screaming at each other. The mother chased her with a broom up and down the stairs and through the house. In order to escape her mother, she would lock herself in the bathroom. I had come down with a bad case of diarrhea so I was constantly waiting at the bathroom door for her to come out. The minute she opened the door I would be inside on the toilet, almost colliding with her. Their fighting and chasing were an ongoing part of my stay there, as was my diarrhea.

I was only allowed outside very early in the morning to take their goat to the meadow. I walked down the still-empty streets, alone with the goat, watching the lights go on in the houses where families were eating breakfast and children were getting ready for school. My loneliness was intense.

vvvvvvvvvv

I was living in a cabin on a lake filled with sailboats. It had the feeling of a resort town. I went grocery shopping with a woman who was warm and lively. When the owner of a store asked her who I was, she told him I was her niece. He exclaimed how much we looked alike.

The Room

The Resistance took me to visit my parents for a weekend. They were hiding in the city of Roermond in the south of Holland, living in an attic room the size of a large closet. This was the first time I had seen them since our separation.

I came from a different world into that tiny room. I had lived with other people and been allowed to go outside. My parents had been confined with each other for twenty-four hours a day. When I entered their room I felt physically bigger. The proportion between us seemed to have changed. Maybe I had grown or maybe the room was so small it could not absorb three people.

There was a bed, one chair, and a small coffee table. Light came through a very narrow window. The bathroom was in the hall. The young children in the family slept in a room right under the attic. Once when my parents forgot to tiptoe, the children heard the noise coming from the attic, and the boogieman was born. Whenever the kids became unmanageable, the mother would threaten them: "If you don't listen the boogieman will come and get you." Somehow she would manage to knock with the handle of a broom against the ceiling, a cue for my parents to stamp their feet.

We played cards all day and all night, and in between they stamped their feet on the floor. Day and night merged.

My mother discovered I had head lice. To treat it, she wrapped a heavy towel soaked in kerosene around my head. It stung badly and smelled worse. I was in a

cocoon removed from everybody.

I felt paralyzed in that tiny room. I don't remember talking, only playing cards and eating. We moved the cards to the bed so we could eat from the coffee table, then moved the coffee table so we could go to bed. The monotony of everything we did is engraved in my memory.

By the time I had to leave, it had become unbearable to be with them. My old normal life seemed never to have existed. I was angry and I felt cornered. I had to come to a decision. I had to stop caring. I felt my only option was to hate my parents. That way I wouldn't have to think about their helplessness or worry about them. My longing for them would diminish.

After my visit I read in the newspaper that the city of Roermond was virtually flattened in a bombing raid. I was terrified until a person from the Resistance told me that only a few buildings escaped destruction and my parents were in one of them. My resolve to hate them crumbled.

Aunts and Uncles

I was told that this family preferred a girl in their home. I was to call the man *Oom* (uncle) Jan and the woman *Tante* (aunt) Hanny. He was an elementary school teacher and she was a housewife. They did not have any children.

I liked *Oom* Jan a lot. He was friendly and easygoing. I liked to read, so he brought me books from his school. *Oom* Jan also brought home the toys he confiscated from boys who were caught playing in the classroom.

Once he brought home a specially made leather pouch. When I opened it, the most beautiful marbles fell out. I couldn't bring myself to play with them because I knew what a great loss it must have been for the child who had owned them. Those marbles could never be mine.

I liked it best when they let me take care of their rabbits. The rabbits were kept in cages with bars on the sides and a bottom made of heavy chicken wire. A removable tray was placed underneath the wire, so the rabbit droppings fell through into the tray. All the cages were whitewashed and very clean. I cut grass for the rabbits with scissors, filling a basket and distributing it evenly. As a treat I picked dandelions for them. With quivering whiskers and soft flaring noses, they ate from my outstretched hand.

Tante Hanny devoted herself to me. I began to feel surrounded by her. She

started telling me about her marriage to *Oom* Jan. She told me in a conspiratorial voice things I couldn't understand. Her manner and tone embarrassed me. I wished she would find someone else to talk to.

Their bathroom did not have a bathtub, just a toilet and washbasin. Bathing was done in the kitchen. Once a week, water was heated and poured into an aluminum tub on the floor. *Tante* Hanny insisted on washing me. Her presence in the kitchen made me uncomfortable, but at the same time I knew that it was my responsibility to be grateful. These people were putting their lives in danger for me.

I told *Tante* Hanny I was too old, that I had been washing myself for a long time. She would not listen. One day the washing turned into a massage. I could not stop her. The expression in her eyes frightened me. In that moment, all my fury at her took over and I splashed her with water. She never touched me again.

〰〰〰〰

Tante Nien and *Oom* Gerrit also lived in the house. They were teachers, and each rented a room. *Oom* Gerrit was tall and thin and *Tante* Nien was small and a little rounded and she smiled a lot. We always had dinner together. They knew I was in hiding and our dinner conversations were mostly political. I began to get a sense of what was going on in the world. There was a radio hidden in the shed. They took turns listening to the BBC and Radio Orange, the secret radio station of the Resistance. This is how we first heard about D day and the British and American landing in France. We knew it was the beginning of our liberation.

One day someone from the Resistance came to tell us that the Germans were planning a raid. They were going to close off the area and search each house for Jews. I was moved to another family until the search was over.

I returned to *Tante* Hanny and *Oom* Jan, but I was no longer allowed to play outside. They would not have been able to explain to the neighbors why I had disappeared during the search for Jews.

We had many air raids at that time, but even then I could not go out. When the alert sounded, everyone except me left the house and went outside to the shelter.

Each alert was always followed by a period of total silence. Alone one night in that silence, waiting for something to happen, I panicked. There was nobody in the house, the streets were empty. I heard the heavy droning of the approaching planes and then all hell broke loose: the ear-shattering crack of antiaircraft artillery, the whiney screeching of planes plunging out of the sky. I ran to the pantry and began grabbing food from the shelves. I ate until I was sick. I was still vomiting when they returned.

I was not punished. I never did it again.

Lieve Truus,

Heb een lied op de lippen,
  Verlies nooit de moed.
Draag de zon in je hartje,
  En alles wordt goed.

tante Nien.

Heerlen, 6 Juni 1944.

aan truusje

weer steeds een vriend'lijk zonne
met helder, stralend licht,
doe je werk op school en thuis
steeds met een blij gezicht
al loopt het soms een keertje te
al dreigt er ook een beetje regen
onthoud maar goed hoe het zal zijn
„na regen komt weer zonneschijn"

ter herinnering aan:
          oom jan de meester.

Dearest Truus,

Have a song on your lips,
Never loose courage
Carry the sun in your heart,
And everything will flourish.

Tante Nien

Heerlen. 6 Juni 1944

Volgt de zonneschijn op regen,
Volgt de vreugd op smart,
Lacht bij het scheiden het weerzien
Als een troost voor het lijdend hart,
Moog dan dit blad tot je spreken
En je zeggen namens mij:
Laat het je nooit aan moed ont-
breken,
Want wat zoveelen tranen leden;
Morgen is het leed voorbij.

Terherinnering aan:

Tante Hanny.

24-5-'44.

For Truusje
Sunshine will follow rain,
As will happiness follow pain,
Smile when parting, because you will meet again,
Use it as a comfort for the suffering heart,
May this page be a start
And let it tell you in my name:
Don't ever loose your courage,
Because what are tears today,
Tomorrow your suffering will have gone away.

Remember me,
Tante Hanny.

24 - 5 '44

verjaardag 1944

poëzie

A poëzie *book is an autograph book in which school children have their classmates and friends write small poems and verses. Since I could not go to school, mostly adults wrote in mine. Nobody was allowed to sign his or her real name; instead they became* Tante *or* Oom *or made up a name. My book starts with "dear Truus." After the war it continues and I become "dear Ruth."*

Tante *Nien wrote her poem on June 6, 1944. She discreetly underlined the date. It was her way of celebrating D day without mentioning it in words, in case the Germans found the book.*

Harm

I don't remember how I got to this house, or what town it was in, or where I had been before. Each place stands alone. It was almost as if I had tried to erase from my memory the family I had to leave in order to go to the next one.

When I arrived I was greeted by what seemed to me dozens of children. Harm was the oldest boy, a little older than me. He had been told that I was Jewish and in hiding. There were at least six other children in this household. One boy stood out. He was younger than me and his hair was jet black. He looked very pale, almost sickly. Harm told me the pale boy was Jewish also, and very smart. He played chess with himself all day. He suffered from a very painful eczema which covered his arms and hands and needed constant care. He never paid attention to any of us. I did not feel any kinship toward him because he was Jewish. I thought he was strange because he never joined us in anything we did. I wondered how he could have been in a public school with regular children. He seemed to live in another world.

Harm told me that another girl had been in hiding with them before I arrived. She had been his girlfriend. When she left, they had made a pact: If she were caught by the Germans and shipped to a concentration camp, then Harm could look for another girlfriend. Harm and I agreed if that happened I would be next in line.

Harm was responsible for his younger siblings. He kept the peace among them and made sure none of his brothers or sisters asked us questions about why we were there or who we were.

The Jewish boy and I were not allowed to go outside. (The rules in each house I lived in were different depending on the circumstances.) One day, after an exceptionally heavy snowstorm, the parents let the two of us go sledding with their own children. It was late in the afternoon and dusk was settling in. They felt nobody would notice two more children all bundled up. Being outside was wonderful. We were having a lot of fun, but the pale boy did not know what to do. He just stood there. Harm was worried that people would notice him, so he took him back to the house. When we came back inside, all excited and warm, the boy was sitting at the table quietly playing his game of chess. He never once looked up.

Harm's family was Protestant. On Sunday everybody would gather around the organ and sing hymns together. It did not matter whether you knew the words. After a while you would get the hang of it and sing along.

There never was quite enough food for us all. The bread was gray and soggy, perfect for making little figures or balls. We were allowed to do that as long as we ate it and did not throw it at each other. I don't remember anyone ever being punished.

Everybody slept in a large attic room, including the parents. We slept two, sometimes three, to a bed. As an only child I had never known anything like it. Everyone belonged; nobody was left behind. There was no room for me to feel isolated.

The parents did not differentiate between their children and us. Everyone was treated the same. This was one family I would have wanted to become part of, but I was afraid of getting too close to them. We would only be separated again. With them in particular, I was much more aware of the chances they took in hiding me. I tried not to think about it. It was too painful to care about them and at the same time to put them in danger. The chances they took were a matter of life and death. I don't even remember their names.

Fall

In one family the mother was having an affair with a man in the Resistance whom I knew as Peter. I don't know how I knew about their affair. I think I had developed an instinct that told me what was going on in each family so I could adjust myself to the role I had to play.

One of my duties with this family was to take their little girl to school every morning. Peter would come by after the husband had left for work and the children had gone to school, so I was not allowed to return to the house until I had picked the girl up in the afternoon. Every day that fall I wandered the streets.

The air was damp and gray and thick layers of leaves covered the sidewalks. The trees were naked and desolate and the flowers were bent and brown. Lamps in the houses were lit early in the afternoon, before the curtains had been drawn. I walked slowly along the sidewalks looking into other people's lives.

The town was in a coal-mining area in the south of Holland. Oily soot from the smokestacks turned the white laundry hanging on lines a dirty gray and even entered the houses through closed windows. No matter where I walked I saw *Lange Jan* (Long John), the tallest smokestack of them all. It looked black against the gray autumn sky. I was told that the direction of its smoke would predict the weather, but I could not figure out where north, east, south, or west was.

wwwwwww

When the family took me in, Peter briefed me about my newest identity. My name was Truus de Bruin. My father was a policeman. My mother had been taken to an insane asylum and my father could not take care of me by himself. I was suffering from TB and therefore could not go to school. (My healthy-looking cheeks worried me, but I was assured that red cheeks could be a symptom of TB.) I was distantly related to the mother but had not visited them for many years. Because of my family's problems, they were taking care of me for a while.

Their son, Wim, who was my age, was small with blond hair and dark eyebrows. His mother spoiled him. He was not told my true identity. I don't think he ever figured out who I was, but he knew something was wrong about my appearing out of nowhere. He kept asking me questions about his family to which only a close relative would have known the answers. Under some pretense I would run to his mother for information and then run back with my reply. His questions kept me in a constant state of anxiety.

I toyed with the idea of telling Wim about his mother and Peter to make him stop pestering me, but the consequences could have been too dangerous. Instead I kept it to myself. It gave me a sense of control over him. I knew that if I could not take his questioning anymore I could always use that power to get back at him.

I remember Wim's mother in a pink robe, which she wore most of the day. It never looked quite clean. Her husband always had his head bent down when walking. He never said much. When there were air raids, he would run down to the cellar at the first sound of the siren. The rest of us would eventually follow.

The mother came down only when the bombs started to fall or when the Germans sent their V-2 rockets to England.

The V-2s made a screaming sound as they passed overhead. If the sound suddenly stopped, it meant the Germans had miscalculated the distance to England and the rocket would explode somewhere nearby. We never got a direct hit, but bombs fell close enough to shatter windows. After the siren signaled all clear, we would scramble out of the cellar to see the damage outside.

Every night at exactly the same time for months and months, squadrons of British and American planes passed high overhead flying toward Germany. Their engines sounded heavy with their loads of bombs. Hours later, when they returned from their mission, they flew lower and faster because they had dropped the bombs. Even the sound of the engines was much lighter. That was when the German fighter planes we called *Jägers* (Hunters) attacked them. Allied planes would come tumbling down through the dark night engulfed in flames. Sometimes we saw parachutes with silhouetted figures hanging underneath floating away from the flames.

wwwwwwww

Peter told me that my parents were hiding nearby and he would take me there for a visit. He insisted it had to be at night so I would not be able to find my way back to them. He did not know how well I knew the village streets from my wanderings. I was not too eager to see my parents. I remembered my last visit.

When I arrived, the first thing my parents spoke about was making a secret plan so I could see them more frequently. They knew I was staying not far from them. The whole idea frightened me. What if someone found out about our scheme? What if I were never allowed to see them again? I was afraid to upset them by showing them my unwillingness. I didn't want to let them down and so I agreed to the plan.

We chose a certain day and hour. Every week I would go to their street and wait until my father's bald head and then his face slowly came up in the bathroom window. If nobody was on the street I would wave and he would wave back. If someone was coming I would raise my eyebrows and he would disappear again. We couldn't speak. My mother never appeared. I never found out why.

I was afraid that some day I might not be able to come at the precise time and my father would be waiting and waiting for me in the bathroom. I don't know how long I kept coming to that corner.

One day my father's head did not appear in the bathroom window. I waited, but he was not there. I kept going back but he never appeared again.

As I wandered through the village, I saw a woman wearing my mother's dress and belt. She looked like the person who had been hiding my parents. I wanted to scream at her: How dare she wear my mother's dress! I was sure the Germans had found my parents. I did not know what to do. Peter was the only one I could ask, but I couldn't let him know I had visited the house. I casually asked him if

my parents were still hiding with the same family. He told me they had learned that their rescuers were selling illegal goods (as many people did during the war to survive) and that the Germans had searched their house several times before. My parents were afraid that the next time the Germans would find them along with all the other illegal goods. They fled in broad daylight, leaving their suitcases behind, and somehow managed to find the house where Peter lived. They must have been terrified to take such a chance.

~~~~~~~~~

More than any other time in hiding, this particular fall stayed with me. I had changed; I had become more afraid of everything around me. There was nobody I could talk to, nobody I could trust.

Liberation

When it became obvious that the liberation was close at hand, my parents begged the Resistance to place us together with one family. They were afraid that during last-minute fighting, shooting, and confusion we would be separated. The Resistance found a family that was willing to take all three of us. Their home was in the village of Brunssum, a half-hour walk across the moor from the German border.

The family lived in a large development of two-story houses. Most of the buildings had been finished, but some were still shells. They had been built by the Germans for the Germans who worked in Holland, as well as for Dutch people who were related to Germans. It actually made it one of the safest places to hide, but I had to be even more cautious since my playmates' parents could be Nazis.

My parents were already at the house when I arrived. They looked pale and seemed very withdrawn. We were like strangers. I could go out anytime I wanted to, but my parents were not allowed to go outside at all. They spent their time in a small upstairs room where I would visit them.

I was torn. I wanted us to be a family again, but I had to force myself to go to their room. When I was with them, we spoke as though nothing much had happened to us. I spent more and more time with the family that owned the house and with their daughter, whose room I shared. It was easier to be with strangers than with my parents.

They only came down to join the family at dinnertime. If the doorbell rang during the meal, my parents pushed back their chairs, picked up their plates, utensils, and napkins, and raced upstairs, avoiding the creaking steps. They were gone in an instant without a trace.

One evening before dinner my father was reading in the dining room when a neighbor walked in. Someone had forgotten to lock the door. My father panicked and slid under the table. The neighbor, very concerned, asked the family what was wrong with this man. They said he had mental problems and could not bear to be around strangers.

I was terrified for my parents, but also angry at them. I hated seeing them running and hiding. I wanted to forget my father running like a thief up the stairs, fork, knife, and plate in hand, or hiding under the table. I hated that they, the adults, were as powerless as I was. When these feelings overwhelmed me I would burst into uncontrollable, unreasonable rages. I had shouting matches with my mother that ended with me crying hysterically. This strange crying, almost without tears, brought me no relief.

Again I tried to remove myself from my parents. I convinced myself that I was adopted, that these people were not my real parents. Deciding I was adopted didn't make me a free person any more than deciding to hate them had. I was still connected to them. They were still my parents.

wwwwwww

The Germans continued to fight their losing battle. As the Allied forces steadily approached, the Germans became more and more frantic. Word got out that they were going to search house by house for males of any age to fight for them in a last desperate effort against the Allies. Both Germans and Dutch fled. It was a strange sight to see every man and boy running out into the moor, trying to hide in the low bushes. My father could barely keep up with the rest. I saw several other men whose faces had the same white pallor as my father's and who had trouble running. I realized they also had been in hiding, but nobody seemed to care anymore. They were all running for their lives. The next day everybody returned safely home.

The Allies advanced slowly, town by town, village by village, and then they arrived in Brunssum. Everyone knew that German snipers were still hiding out, but nevertheless the streets were lined with people. The first tanks approached, rolling very slowly, their enormous metal treads moving like caterpillars. The tanks were sealed shut with just the ends of machine guns sticking out, ready to shoot. It was menacing. Were our liberators really inside those prehistoric monsters?

After what seemed like a long time, the tanks opened up and, one by one, American soldiers started to emerge. They threw chewing gum, candy, and cigarettes down to us. In one big surge we surrounded them, urging them to come down so we could hug them. They didn't. They probably were not allowed to. Instead they waved and smiled at us as we danced along beside the slow-moving tanks. The infantry came next. They were marching but they did not in the least resemble the goose-stepping Germans we were used to. Theirs was an easy, from-the-hips marching, and they smiled at us as they went by. That was the moment my admiration for the Americans started. A country that could produce an army like that must be a glorious place to live.

wwwwwww

Now we were liberated, but we had no place to live. The Dutch authorities and the Americans gave us permission to move into one of the many now-abandoned houses in the development. German families had fled across the moor to Germany, leaving everything behind. We took our time going through different houses, stepping into other people's lives again. In one we did not like the furniture. In another the house was not well kept. Finally we found a house my parents thought was livable. The furniture was dark and heavy and overstuffed. A couple and their daughter must have lived there. Her bedroom had all the things I liked, especially a vanity with a full-length mirror, lots of drawers, and a chair. We moved in, but continued to live out of our suitcases.

My father found a job in the American kitchen. It was a coveted job. The Americans, besides being very generous, had the reputation of throwing out food that was barely touched. If one sausage was spoiled, the whole link was thrown out, though the rest were perfectly all right. As a result, we and our neighbors had plenty to eat during that time.

My father was a heavy smoker and never had enough cigarettes. When armies from Canada and England came through I would follow any soldier who was smoking. When he threw away the stub I immediately picked it up. My father took the tobacco and re-rolled his own cigarettes. Very quickly I figured out that it was a waste of time to follow Canadian or English soldiers. Only the Americans threw away half a cigarette.

The Americans marched and exercised on our street. The drill sergeant had a girlfriend on our block and made his men do all their maneuvers in front of her house. One division was black soldiers only. I watched them every morning and thought America a wondrous and exotic country.

In the afternoons after school I would walk along the streets where the American soldiers lived in the unfinished houses. They played heartfelt music that was repetitive and full of anguish. I could almost understand the simple lyrics. I made up my mind. One day I would go to America where soldiers walked with a casual freedom like regular people, and listened to music I could relate to—country and western.

The American army soon moved on and my father had to look for a more permanent job. In Germany he had been a traveling salesman, so he tried to find the same kind of work in Holland. We never realized how difficult it would be for him going from door to door. Hatred of the Germans was so strong in Holland that when Dutch people heard my father's heavy accent, they slammed the door. He wasn't given even a minute to explain that he was Jewish as well as German.

One day my father and I came upon a group of people who were holding three women against their will. These women had been involved with German soldiers, and their captors were shaving their heads to humiliate them. A crowd was egging them on.

My father looked horrified, and then very angry. He pushed his way through the crowd. In spite of his poor Dutch and thick German accent, he told the men they were no better than the Germans. I remember the dead silence that followed.

wwwwwww

I went back to school again. I had missed two years while I was in hiding but, thanks to the books that *Oom* Jan had lent me, I was held back only one year. In reading I wasn't behind at all.

Southern Holland is mostly Catholic so I went to a Catholic elementary school. I was the only Jewish student and the nuns were extremely nice to me. Sister Angele introduced me to the class as the person who had just come out of hiding. I did not know what to say. The other children did not know either, so we never spoke about the war and hiding. We continued our lives.

My family had very little clothing left after the war. Once we were able to contact our relatives in the United States again, we started to receive lots of clothes. For some reason nobody thought of sending me socks. It was summer, so I could go to school in sandals and bare feet. I liked the feeling of bare toes, and I knew the nuns could not berate me because I had no socks to wear. Sister Angele and the other nuns were very upset. It was indecent for girls to expose their calves. We were supposed to wear socks that covered them.

They decided I could not possibly continue looking like a heathen. Without my knowledge they asked each child to bring a ball of cotton yarn, any color, to school and from these the nuns knitted for me the most colorful socks. They even put elastic at the tops to keep them from sliding down my almost nonexistent calves. The socks really stood out and I loved them. After hiding for so long, standing out made me feel good. I was visible again.

My mother encouraged me to feel good about the socks, saying that being different was something to be proud of. I remembered the feeling of being cared for. My mother was there; she listened to me and gave me advice. I was included again.

Going to Catholic school made a deep impression on me. The saints were there to help you with every possible problem. You could cheat in school and ask forgiveness. After a couple of Hail Marys, it was granted. It seemed so simple and easy. The churches were beautiful with their dazzling stained-glass windows. Catholicism was all around me, but I didn't have any strong feelings for it.

My mother had grown up in a religious household. She made me promise never to forget that I was Jewish. She would talk to me about her family preparing for the Jewish high holidays, her voice full of longing and sadness. It seemed like a very distant memory to her.

I was very aware of my Jewishness. After all, it had been the reason for the years of hiding. I didn't have any strong feelings for Judaism either, and I didn't know anyone who was practicing it. It seemed I was lacking a sense of religion all together.

Jimmy

The Americans moved on and the English and Canadians settled in. The English almost goose-stepped when they marched, an unpleasant reminder of the very recent past. Their lieutenants and other officers moved into people's homes, rather than into the unfinished houses like the ordinary soldiers.

A lieutenant from Scotland was assigned to us. He was quite different from the other English officers. He did not have a personal servant-soldier to shine his shoes and take care of him as the others did.

His name was Jimmy, and he came from Glasgow. He had a son there who had been born while he was fighting the war. He had been at the front for quite a while, long enough to be delighted to sit in an armchair and enjoy lamplight. He was gone during the day and came back every night to our house. I was allowed to stay up and wait for him. We were able to communicate with each other even though my English was nonexistent.

Jimmy had fought in the Spanish Civil War. He taught me to sing in Spanish "La Paloma," a song from that war. He recited poetry to me in words that did not sound like English, but had a lilt and beauty I had never heard before. Maybe it was his Scottish accent or maybe it was the emotion he put into it, but I understood the feelings even though I could not understand his words. He also took me to the movies. No other thirteen year old that I knew was escorted by a lieutenant to the movies. I felt quite special and grown-up.

The Germans had not completely given up their last vestiges of resistance. We still had air raids and Jimmy joined us when we went down to our basement for shelter.

Jimmy was ordered to go back to the front again. He was weary and tired of the war. He didn't want to go. When he said good-bye he wrote in my *poëzie* book.

A couple of days later we were notified that he had been killed in action.

GEMEENTE H
VOORLOOPIG PA

(voor repatrieerenden e

Naam: Katzenstein, echtgen

Voornamen: Paula

Geboortedatum: 3 November

Geboorteplaats: Frankenberg,

Beroep: zonder

Nationaliteit: Statenloos

Godsdienst: NI

Adres: Hermelijnstraat H 6 7

Heerlen, 26 September   1944.

Voor den Burgemeester,
De Chef van het Bevolkingsbureau,

Peace

At last the war was over. Armies no longer marched through our streets. Soldiers no longer went to the front. People tried to return to their normal lives, but my parents never could. The years of hiding had damaged them somehow and peace didn't end their torment.

My mother was now tired all the time. She no longer had the energy to have a real conversation with me. My father had found work traveling around the country assisting a Dutch salesman, so he was gone a lot of the time. When he was home, he spent his evenings playing cards in the neighborhood bar. We had very little money. We could not pay our bills and this brought on many arguments.

My mother was suffering from depression, and every year it became worse. By the time I was in high school, she could not take care of the house anymore. She had always loved cooking, but even that became too much for her. My father had to hire a housekeeper.

I took my mother to a constant stream of different doctors and psychiatrists. Once, we even tried a hypnotist in Amsterdam. We went by train and stayed overnight in a hotel. Amsterdam was a cosmopolitan city. I should have been excited to be there, but all I felt was fear at having to stay in the same room with her.

I was uncomfortable being in her room at home, too. She was always resting. It was always dark. The air felt heavy and my breathing became shallow. I

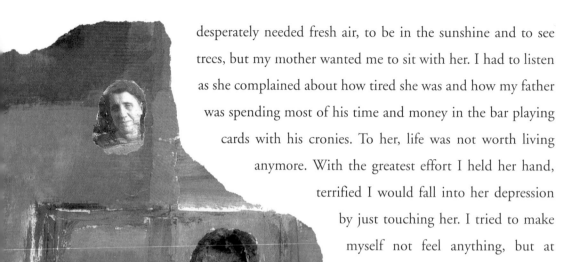

desperately needed fresh air, to be in the sunshine and to see trees, but my mother wanted me to sit with her. I had to listen as she complained about how tired she was and how my father was spending most of his time and money in the bar playing cards with his cronies. To her, life was not worth living anymore. With the greatest effort I held her hand, terrified I would fall into her depression by just touching her. I tried to make myself not feel anything, but at night when I could not sleep, I would sneak a look at her to make sure she was still breathing.

Hypnosis didn't work. She became more depressed and had trouble sleeping. She tried sleeping pills and quickly became dependent on them. She took more pills, but slept even less, and was groggy most of the time. She heard of something quite new and decided to try it: electric shock treatments.

The doctors at that time knew very little about the effect it had on patients. They hospitalized her in order to give her the shock treatments, but gave her such high doses and so many treatments that it started to affect her heart. They stopped the high doses but she continued treatments as an outpatient a couple of days a week.

I would take her on the bus to the hospital and wait for her in the hallway outside the treatment room. The door would open and someone would push her out. Dazed, her shoes in her hand and her coat over her arm, my mother would just stand there. I would help her dress and take her home again on the bus. My life centered around my mother.

My father rarely was at home. I never asked him why. I didn't want to know. I just wanted him to talk to me about helping my mother.

Instead he talked to Roosje, the housekeeper. I knew for certain I was in the same situation I had been in with Wim's mother, but now it was my own father who was having the affair. I was sure my mother knew also, though she never talked about it. She, who could not cope with life's simplest demands, was confronted every day with Roosje and my father.

It was all too much for her. She took an overdose of sleeping pills. I was not the one who found her—someone else called the ambulance—but I did see her lying still in bed. It was the kind of stillness I had been afraid of finding when I would sneak a look at her at night.

She survived the overdose and was taken to an asylum where she stayed for several weeks. When she came home again, my parents decided to file for a divorce. The plan was that my mother and I would emigrate to America to join her brother and sisters. My mother had no money and neither did my father, and I earned very little. Even if we had had enough money, apartments were hard to find. We had no choice but to live together until we got permission to emigrate, which could take as long as a year.

I wanted to get Roosje out of the house. I confronted my father and gave him an ultimatum: Either Roosje leaves or I leave. My father, without hesitation, told me to get out.

After I had graduated from high school, I found a job as a counselor in a Children's Home. I could live in the Home, but that left my mother alone with Roosje and my father.

Tante Marie came to her rescue. She and her husband had hidden my parents during the war and the two women had become close. *Tante* Marie invited my mother to live with them until we could leave for America. She gladly accepted.

〜〜〜〜〜〜〜

On May 17, 1952, a policeman came to the Children's Home and asked for me. He told me that my mother had died and that I needed to identify her. He did not tell me what had happened and I did not ask. I have no memory of the ride to the police station.

When we arrived at the station, a door was opened and I saw my mother lying there. In a flash I saw her face and her legs stretched out silently. I was oddly relieved that she was dressed, but wondered why her face was so yellow. I could not look at her for another second. I turned abruptly and made for the door. That was the last time I saw her. I don't remember my father being there.

Tante Marie told me that my mother had seemed all right that day. She had taken a bus to a neighboring village. A couple of hours after she left, an errand boy came to *Tante* Marie's house to tell her that she had a phone call. (People did not have telephones in their homes then. They received phone calls at the

drugstore or grocer.) It took a while for *Tante* Marie to get to the phone. By that time the person had hung up. We were pretty certain that it had been my mother trying to call *Tante* Marie at the last minute. It was around that time that the police pulled her from the village pond.

I was not allowed to go to the burial, and there was no funeral service. In the Jewish religion a person who commits suicide is buried without rituals.

The day after my mother's death I went to the convent for my weekly English lesson with Sister Calasancta. I had known her since high school. She was head of the school, and taught English, Dutch, and writing. She had been strict, but not stifling, and encouraged questions which was unheard of in that time and place. She took an interest in me, and I escaped from the pain of my family life to her safe, calm presence.

She was seated in the garden when I arrived, her hands tucked into her sleeves. She raised her eyebrows in surprise when I appeared, and gazed at me with her commanding, marble-shaped eyes. I was mute, and she did not say anything. She must have understood that the peace in that garden was saving my life. We began our lesson.

Tante Marie also understood and comforted me without words. I spent occasional weekends with her, and every night she served me hot oatmeal. It soothed me into a relaxed sleep.

I never cried after my mother's death. I could not talk about it to anyone for fear that my grief would engulf me.

A few months later I received permission to emigrate. I had to make a decision. It was out of the question to stay in the Children's Home; my father and Roosje lived too near. I could either live in Amsterdam or go to America. I had no real sense of distance. A trip to Amsterdam (a two-hour train ride) seemed no different to me than a trip to America. I decided I might as well go to America.

I left from Rotterdam on January 17, 1953. *Tante* Marie came to the pier to see me off with a bag of apples. She made me promise to eat them so I would not get seasick. My father and Roosje came also. I didn't want to see them, but I managed a stiff and formal good-bye.

The Atlantic crossing took ten days. The meals were the most interesting part. An American couple sat at my table in the dining room. My English was good enough that I could understand them, but I was too shy to speak. I watched instead the complicated way they used their utensils. They held their meat with a fork and cut a bite-size piece with a knife. Then they placed the knife horizontally on the far edge of the plate, changed the fork from the left hand to the right hand, and finally ate. I was determined to learn how to do that by the end of the voyage.

The evening before our arrival everyone ran to the deck. I saw what looked like a small brightly lit city, with a gigantic Ferris wheel glittering in the night. I was told this was Coney Island. It was America welcoming me to start a new life.

wwwwwww

Once I arrived in America I answered my father's letters as briefly as possible. I didn't have much to say to him. He had married Roosje after I left.

Then I received a letter. This is the translation.

Treebeek 22/4 '54

Dearest Ruth,

I am very sorry that after two years you are receiving this strange letter. However, my mind is peaceful knowing that things are going well for you in the new world and you certainly will find your way. Financially I hit rock bottom. When everything is sold it probably will just cover the debts. I gave my wedding ring to Roosje and hope she will keep my last wish to give it to you. Remain brave and don't give up. I finish for the last time with much love.

your father

Immediately I sent a telegram to *Tante* Marie. Of course it was too late. My father had committed suicide on April 23, 1954, the day after he wrote to me.

wwwwwwww

Five years later, I went back to Europe to visit my parents' graves. They were located in the Jewish section of a cemetery, a quiet area separate from the main Catholic part. Some of the headstones had inscriptions in memory of people who had died in concentration camps. *Auschwitz, 1943. Buchenwald, 1942. Westerbork, 1942.* It seemed fitting that my parents' graves were among them. The Nazis had killed them as surely as if they had died in a camp.

I did not cry, but the nausea and dull pain in my head felt as if I had been crying for a long time.

I drove around Heerlen trying to find the streets I used to live on, but I was completely turned around and confused. Nothing looked familiar. My mind was a blank. All I wanted was to go back to America, where I did not have to face the past.

Treebeek, 22/4.54

Lieve Ruth!

Het spijt mij ontzettend dat je na twee jaren al weer zo een rare brief krijgt. Ook ik ben het moe, nog een dag langer alles mee te maken. Ik kon nu beginnen een grote klaag-lijst op te stellen. Toch wil van alles dit afzien. Wel ben ik rustig, in de gedachte dat het je in de nieuwe wereld goed gaat en je verder je weg zeker vinden zult.

HIER RUSTEN
MIJN LIEVE OUDERS
PAULA JACOBSEN
GEB. KATZENSTEIN
+ 3.11.1899
† 17.5.1952
WALTER JACOBSEN
+ 3.12.1900
† 23.4.1954

financiël ben ik heden totaal
je de grond. als alles verkocht is zal wel niet
genoeg zijn om de schulden te betalen.
Mijn Trouwring heb voor jou aan Roosje over-
handigt en hoop ik, dat zij mij deze laatste
belofte houdt en aan jou overmaakt.
    Ruth het ga je goed en blijf dapper
je doorzetten. Ik eindige voor het laatste
met vele lieve groeten.
                    Je Vader.

Alle dingen, die achter de rug
zijn, uit te gaan bannen of
bouwend te werk gaan met alle
zorgen, die er nog zijn en correct
treten op actie, niet op bedoni
wing

Handteekening van
gerechtigde:

Paula Jacobsen – Katzenstein

RLEN.
OONSBEWIJS.

ondergedokenen

te van Jacobs

ⁱⁱⁱⁱⁱ

uitschland

Remembering

My mother's voice was so distinctive that years after she died I could still imagine it. I couldn't actually hear it in my ears, but in the back of my head I could remember the low, pleasant quality of her voice.

Before the war she used to sing me to sleep. After the war my mother taught me the entire *Three Penny Opera*. She told me it was my legacy and it should not be forgotten. Because its creators, Kurt Weil and Bertold Brecht, were Jewish, the Nazis called the opera degenerate. They burned it in a public square.

She taught me *The Three Penny Opera,* but never sang it with me. The freedom she used to feel when singing had gone. After the war I never heard her sing again.

One night, many years after she died, I heard my mother's voice. I was sleeping when I heard her say, "Ruth." I answered, "Yes?" which woke me up. Her voice was so close and clear that it sounded as if she were right next to me. I got out of bed and looked for her, but there was no one there.

It was a dream but it was real. It was her voice. The war years and all the time in between had been pushed aside. She was her calm and loving self again.

I keep a small, framed picture of my mother in my studio. It reminds me of her voice.

Ellen

Just after the war ended, *Tante* Marie arrived at our house with a rather large box. It was for me. I opened it and there was Ellen, my doll. I had to leave her with my parents when I went into hiding by myself. She had been taken from me just as my parents had been taken from me. Ellen was a piece of the past. I had missed her, but had buried her deep in my memory.

She had a realistic baby's face. My mother told me that she was one of the few dolls made so well. I loved just looking at her. She had stamped on the base of her neck a trademark in the shape of a turtle and the brand name *Schildkrote* (turtle). When we were still living in Germany, my aunt had crocheted a whole wardrobe for her. Her pajamas were made from the same material as mine.

After my parents had moved to many different families, they decided to leave Ellen with *Tante* Marie for safekeeping. *Tante* Marie put her into a china display case. Every night her two little boys were allowed to hold Ellen and kiss her goodnight. They called her Paula, my mother's name, because they had grown so fond of her.

One night while being held, Ellen accidentally fell to the floor. Her porcelain head shattered completely. *Tante* Marie picked up each tiny piece and carefully glued them all back together again, an almost impossible task.

I didn't know about the accident, but when I slipped off her beautiful crocheted hat I saw the most incredible thing. The top of her head was perfectly shaped, but had been transformed into a mosaic, each piece fitting next to the other.

Thinking about Ellen many years later, I knew why I had so often used dolls in my collages. It was Ellen over and over again: her head broken, glued together with a beautiful hat to cover the many pieces, the shape of the head intact.

Afterword

Most of the "aunts" and "uncles" who risked their lives to hide me were lost to me as soon as I left their homes, but I was able to contact a few of my rescuers after the war. After I became an American citizen, I would periodically return to Holland to visit Cees van Bart, Tante Marie, and Sister Calasancta.

On my first visit, Cees brought me to the house my family had gone to our first night of hiding. I did not recognize the house and he did not tell me where we were. When we went up to the second floor and looked out the window, I knew. It was the same window through which I had watched my friends playing while I was in hiding. I became agitated and came down with a violent attack of diarrhea. We left and didn't come back. Cees had no idea I would react that way. He thought I would be interested to see this piece of my past.

I did not talk about my wartime experiences with my rescuers. I had less hesitation asking them about what had happened to them during the war. It was easier than thinking about my own past. I wanted to know how they had survived and why they had risked their lives for others. I asked about their memories of my parents, and the more they told me, the more I wanted to know.

Some of my questions had to do with simple curiosity. But looking back, I think it was more. Through my rescuers' memories, the darkness that was my past began to have an outline. I believe that, without knowing, I was preparing myself for the day, many years later, when I would open the albums and look at my family's photographs. Thanks to my rescuers, and the friendship of their children, I've slowly been able to put together the painful pieces of my past.

Baron and Baroness van Tuyll van Serooskerken

The Baron and Baroness van Tuyll van Serooskerken believed that as Christians it was their duty to help people in need. They were active with the Dutch Red Cross and were in the Dutch Resistance. To this day, people in Oud Zuylen claim that there is a tunnel beneath the castle that the Resistance used for transporting people and weapons, but I have not found anybody who actually knows, or will tell, where it is.

The baron died in 1958. The castle where he welcomed us and where we lived for ten days has become a national museum and is open to the public. The baroness lived in the gardener's cottage on the castle grounds until her death in 1978.

Recently I was able to locate one of their daughters, the younger of the two Freules that I played with in the little toy house. She was as excited as I when we started to write to each other. We are still trying to piece together what each of us remembers from that time.

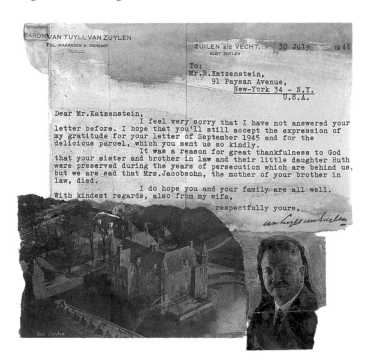

BARON VAN TUYLL VAN ZUYLEN
TEL. MAARSSEN K. 3408/407

ZUILEN a/d VECHT, 30 July 1946
SLOT ZUYLEN

To:
Mr.R.Katzenstein,
91 Paysan Avenue,
New-York 34 - N.Y.
U.S.A.

Dear Mr.Katzenstein,
    I feel very sorry that I have not answered your letter before. I hope that you'll still accept the expression of my gratitude for your letter of September 1945 and for the delicious parcel, which you sent us so kindly.
    It was a reason for great thankfulness to God that your sister and brother in law and their little daughter Ruth were preserved during the years of persecution which are behind us, but we are sad that Mrs.Jacobsohn, the mother of your brother in law, died.
    I do hope you and your family are all well.
With kindest regards, also from my wife,
    respectfully yours,

Slot Zuylen

Cees and Co van Bart

Cees van Bart, the man who saved our photo albums, and our lives, was a quiet hero. When once I asked him if he felt that what he had done was heroic he said simply, "I didn't think about it. I just did what was right in the situation."

I began writing to Cees and his wife, Co, after my parents died. We became close friends, but hardly ever mentioned the war. It wasn't until after his death that his daughter, Janny, told me what had happened to him and Co during those years.

After he had placed us in hiding, Cees was forced to work in a labor camp in Germany making airplanes for the Nazis. He had nightmares until the day he died because of the severe beatings he suffered there. He and other assembly line workers found ways to sabotage planes. During test flights the planes crashed immediately upon take off. The Germans could not find the culprits, so they selected a husband and wife at random from the camp and shot them as a warning. Cees, realizing the danger he was in, managed to escape back to Holland. He went into hiding himself with a farm family.

The Germans regularly searched for deserters as well as Jews. During one wintertime search Cees jumped into a river and held onto an overhanging tree branch. By the time the couple who owned the farm came to tell him the danger was over, he was stiff from the cold and could not move. They had to pull him from the water.

During another search he hid in a shed. He lay down on the straw-covered cement floor. The couple piled straw on top of him and put a goat on top of the straw. Cees held on to the goat's front legs so that it couldn't move until the search was over.

Even while hiding himself, Cees helped others. He transported Jews to different hiding places and stole food ration stamps at post offices to distribute to people in hiding. Co also risked her life to help people escape.

Cees told me before he died that there was one thing he felt sad about. Of all the people he transported to safety, he only heard from my family. He never knew if any of the others survived.

Tante Marie

I met Tante Marie and her husband, Pa Jansen, just after the war. Like Cees, they never thought for a minute that they were being brave in hiding my parents. They saw people in need and acted to help them. Tante Marie, I thought, had the capacity to care for the whole world. Her face radiated kindness.

Pa Jansen was a railroad worker and a man of few words. Tante Marie was the opposite. She and my mother had long conversations about politics and books. When she first visited us after the war, she brought a small oil painting my mother had admired while hiding in her house. I still have it and am quite attached to it.

I got to know Tante Marie after my mother's death and I understood why she and my mother got along so well. Her understanding and compassion were boundless. She became my family.

Sister Calasancta

FEESTELIJKHEDEN ROND AFSCHEID
VAN ZUSTER CALASANCTA

I think of Sister Calasancta as a rescuer, even though she never hid me or my parents during the war. She rescued me emotionally during the very difficult years after the war.

Sister Calasancta and I started our correspondence when I emigrated to America and continued it until her death thirty-seven years later. Year after year, in her fine handwriting she shared her thoughts and feelings. She was a deeply religious person but never interfered in the nonreligious life that I had chosen for myself. At first we wrote in English. Later she suggested that we use Dutch so I would not forget the language.

The last time I saw Sister Calasancta was in 1985. She was living in a convent for retired nuns. She was suffering from heart disease and cancer and looked frail. Despite her illness, she was still lively, full of passion. She had always loved politics and was an early supporter of the women's movement. During dinner in a nearby town she expressed her indignation over American politics of the Reagan years. Her fierceness of character, which I always admired, had not diminished.

She showed me the cemetery where she was to be buried. The rows of identical white crosses made it look like a battlefield cemetery. The inscriptions bore only the nun's religious name and the number of years she had served Jesus Christ. Sister Calasancta, with her arms folded across her chest, surveyed the small cemetery with a peaceful expression on her face. I envied her.

We said our good-byes. As always, she asked me to send her books. It was Judaism she was interested in this time. She died in 1990.

In 1997, I went back to visit her grave. A nun took me to the cemetery. Every grave was covered with an abundance of marigolds, a blanket of orange and yellow. The nun found Sister Calasancta's grave, crossed herself, and kneeled to pray. I bent and pulled the wilted flowers from each plant so new ones could bloom in their place. The pungent scent of marigolds stayed on my hands for a long time.

I have always portrayed Sister Calasancta in collages and on canvas as a fierce bird sheltering me under its wings. She was, and still is, my fearless protector. I will always miss her, not with regret, but with the knowledge that if there should be a God and heaven, she is there, praying for me.

Acknowledgements

I would like to thank:

Miranda D'Ancona, one of my first and truest friends in this country, for her capacity to listen and her sage advice.

Blanche Wiesen Cook, for suggesting that I put art and text into book form and for telling me that I could do it.

Ann Grifalconi, for her enthusiasm and advice, and for giving me the courage to keep going.

Selma Lanes, for reading the book in the beginning, for her suggestions and for giving me the confidence to keep working on it.

Doris Kaufman, for her comments and suggestions which were always appreciated.

The participants at my first writing workshop, for giving me the freedom to start writing.

The participants at my last writing workshop, for listening so carefully and for their comments and suggestions which were always right on the mark. They educated me about the publishing world.

Stu Waldman and Livvie Mann, my editors and publishers, for their sensitivity and understanding and for their patience with me when I needed to talk in order to write about my jumbled emotions.

Janny van Bart, in Holland, for tirelessly hunting down events in the past that I needed to have clarified. Her liveliness and interest were infectious. She has become family.

Molly, my cat, for sitting with me as I wrote, her head on my arm, purring, giving me warmth and reassurance.

Chris, my partner, for her patience and understanding.

Since emigrating to the United States in 1953, Ruth Jacobsen has worked in various jobs ranging from textile designer to motion picture projectionist. She began creating her collages and constructions in the mid sixties. For the last three decades, she has exhibited them in both solo and group shows. Her work is represented in 30 private collections in the United States, Canada and Europe.

Ruth Jacobsen works from her home in Southhampton, New York.

Linz n. d. 10. Januar 1940

Meine Lieben! Wir glaubten schon Ihr hättet uns vergessen und haben uns mit deinem Brief l. Selma sehr gefreut. Es tut mir leid, dass sich dein altes Leiden wieder bemerkbar macht, ich dachte, das hättest du längst überwunden. In den letzten Jahren ging es doch ganz gut? Nun zuerst zu deinem Geburtstage alles Gute und die besten Wünsche. Ja, jünger werden wir alle nicht, aber ich glaube, wenn man an die "Fünfzig" kommt, merkt man erst, dass die Zeit nicht stillgestanden hat. Die Verheiratung von Hilde hat mich sehr überrascht, und wünsche ich den Beiden das denkbar Beste zu ihrem jungen Glück. Euch Beiden, dass Ihr recht bald Oma und Opa gerufen werdet. Für deine Wünsche zu meinem Geburtstage danke ich herzlich, gute Wünsche kann man immer gebrauchen. Dein Brief war über 4 Wochen unterwegs, er ist durch die englische Zensur gegangen. Wir wohnen nun schon ½ Jahr hier. Uns geht es nicht nur gut, sondern mehr als glänzend. Wir wohnen nicht, wie in Deutschland damals angegeben Haus Zinglenbeld, sondern der Baron hat uns ein wunder-schönes Häuschen, das vollständig renoviert wurde, vollständig eingerichtet. Aber davon nachher noch mehr. —